FUCK YOU SUN

by Matt Cole
Pictures by Rigel Stuhmiller

With thanks to Jason Sweeney
Copyright 2011 by Tomorrow John Press
www.tomorrowjohn.com

Am I in my room?
Where'd I put my phone?
Man, it's almost noon.
What's this picture of?

It's me acting like a buffoon

There were three-dollar beers at that place on the pier

And too little water.
And my boss's daughter?

And a little red dress.
And a nasty mess.

And a wink and a grope and a bowl full of dope,

And a creepy old hobo with a belt made of rope.

Fuck you, booze

Fuck you, weird sticky shit on my shoes

Fuck you, lack of self-control

And stupid quarterly revenue goal

Fuck you, garbage truck

And you, leaf blower

And fuck this shit strewn
all over the floor.

Fuck you, clock

And mismatched sock.

Gah, did I hook up with *them*?

Fuck you, three to four a.m.

Made in the USA
Middletown, DE
19 June 2015